Contents

For attention of the learner

You are not allowed to copy any information from this book and use it as your own evidence. That would count as plagiarism, which is taken very seriously and may result in disqualification. If you are in any doubt at all please speak to your teacher.

Command words

You will find the following command words in the assessment criteria for each unit.

Compare and contrast	Identify the main factors relating to two or more items/situations, and explain the similarities and differences, and in some cases say which is best and why.
Describe	Give a clear description that includes all the relevant features – think of it as 'painting a picture with words'.
Evaluate	Bring together all the information and review it to form a conclusion. Give evidence for each of your views or statements.
Explain	Provide details and give reasons and/or evidence to support the arguments being made. Start by introducing the topic then give the 'how' or 'why'.
Justify	Give reasons or evidence to support opinion, to show how conclusions have been arrived at.
Lead	Take charge of others in an activity or situation.
Plan	Work out how you would carry out a task or activity.
Review	Examine a topic or an item to make sure that it is correct or to provide a report on the quality of a document/report/item.

BTEC
SPORT

ASSESSMENT GUIDE

Unit 6 LEADING SPORTS ACTIVITIES

ANDREW BARDSLEY

Edited by
Jennifer Stafford-Brown & Simon Rea

HODDER
EDUCATION
AN HACHETTE UK COMPANY

The sample learner answers provided in this assessment guide are intended to give guidance on how a learner might approach generating evidence for each assessment criterion. Answers do not necessarily include all of the evidence required to meet each assessment criterion. Assessor comments intend to highlight how sample answers might be improved to help learners meet the requirements of the grading criterion but are provided as a guide only. Sample answers and assessor guidance have not been verified by Edexcel and any information provided in this guide should not replace your own internal verification process.

Any work submitted as evidence for assessment for this unit must be the learner's own. Submitting as evidence, in whole or in part, any material taken from this guide will be regarded as plagiarism. Hodder Education accepts no responsibility for learners plagiarising work from this guide that does or does not meet the assessment criteria.

The sample assignment briefs are provided as a guide to how you might assess the evidence required for all or part of the internal assessment of this Unit. They have not been verified or endorsed by Edexcel and should be internally verified through your own Lead Internal Verifier as with any other assignment briefs, and/or checked through the BTEC assignment checking service.

The authors and publishers would like to thank the following for the use of photographs in this volume:

Figure 1.1 Christophe Fouquin – Fotolia; Figure 1.2 Monkey Business – Fotolia; Figure 1.4 burak çakmak – Fotolia; Figure 1.5 Lorraine Swanson – Fotolia; Figure 1.6 © Bob Daemmrich / Alamy; Figure 1.7 Brian Jackson – Fotolia; Figure 1.8 Andrew Powell/Liverpool FC via Getty Images; Figure 1.9 © ALAIN VERMEULEN – Fotolia; Figure 1.10 Michael Flippo – Fotolia; Figure 1.11 Dusan Kostic – Fotolia; Figure 2.1 Nottingham Trent University; Figure 2.2 .shock – Fotolia; Figure 2.3 mills21 – Fotolia; Figure 3.1 Ross Land/Getty Images; Figure 3.2 Dmitry Naumov – Fotolia

Every effort has been made to trace and acknowledge ownership of copyright. The publishers will be glad to make suitable arrangements with any copyright holders whom it has not been possible to contact.

Orders: please contact Bookpoint Ltd, 130 Milton Park, Abingdon, Oxon OX14 4SB. Telephone: (44) 01235 827720. Fax: (44) 01235 400454. Lines are open from 9.00–5.00, Monday to Saturday, with a 24 hour message answering service. You can also order through our website www.hoddereducation.co.uk

If you have any comments to make about this, or any of our other titles, please send them to educationenquiries@hodder.co.uk

British Library Cataloguing in Publication Data

A catalogue record for this title is available from the British Library

ISBN: 978 1 444 1 86741

Published 2013

Impression number   10 9 8 7 6 5 4 3 2 1

Year   2016 2015 2014 2013

Copyright © 2013 Andrew Bardsley, Jennifer Stafford-Brown and Simon Rea

Cover photo © Africa Studio – Fotolia

Typeset by Integra Software Services Pvt. Ltd., Pondicherry, India

Printed in Dubai for Hodder Education,
an Hachette UK Company,
338 Euston Road,
London NW1 3BH

Introduction

Unit 6, Leading Sports Activities, is an internally assessed, optional, specialist unit with three learning aims:

- Learning aim A: Know the attributes associated with successful sports leadership
- Learning aim B: Undertake the planning and leading of sports activities
- Learning aim C: Review the planning and leading of sports activities.

The unit focuses on sports leadership, covering the basics then asking you to plan and deliver a sports session and evaluate your own leadership. Learning aim A covers the attributes of successful sports leaders and learning aim B looks at the planning and leadership of sports sessions. In learning aim C you evaluate your leadership performance in the session you planned and delivered, assessing your own strengths and weaknesses.

Each learning aim is divided in to two sections. The first section focuses on the content of the learning aim and each of the topics are covered. At the end of each learning aim there are some knowledge recap questions to test your understanding of the subject. The answers for the knowledge recap questions can be found at the end of the book.

The second section of each learning aim provides assessment support by using evidence generated by a student, for each grading criterion, with feedback from an assessor. The assessor has highlighted where the evidence is sufficient to satisfy the grading criterion and provided developmental feedback when additional work is required.

At the end of the book is an example of an assignment brief for this unit. The sample assignment brief contains tasks that would allow you to generate the evidence needed to meet all the assessment criteria in the unit. The assessment criteria are also outlined in a table following the brief.

Learning aim A
Know the attributes associated with successful sports leaders

Assessment criteria

(2A.P1)	Describe, using relevant examples, the attributes required for, and responsibilities of, sports leadership.
(2A.M1)	Explain the attributes required for, and responsibilities of, sports leadership.
(2A.P2)	Describe the attributes of two selected successful sports leaders.
(2A.M2)	Evaluate the attributes of two successful sports leaders.
(2A.D1)	Compare and contrast the attributes of two successful sports leaders.

Topic A.1 Sports leaders

Figure 1.1 Sports leaders play a vital role

Sports leaders play a vital role in developing skills, improving performance levels and providing motivation to sports performers. The growth in popularity of sport and leisure activities has meant that more people are needed to run a variety of different sports sessions such as after school clubs and voluntary sports clubs. Examples of the types of sports leaders there are include sports coaches, fitness instructors, school/college coaches, local club coaches, national club coaches and amateur coaches.

Topic A.2 Attributes

A range of skills and qualities is required to plan and lead sports sessions and events which can be developed through practice. As well as having the correct skills and qualities, there are many responsibilities that fall upon the leader.

Skills

Communication

Communication is the exchange of information between two people and is one of the most important skills for any sports leader. However, good communication skills are difficult to master. There are several ways a leader can communicate in a sporting environment:

Figure 1.2 Communicating in a sporting environment

1. Verbal communication – it is important to speak clearly so that the participants can clearly understand what you are telling them. You should avoid using too many technical words and use language that is suited to the participant. You should try to use positive comments to increase motivation as critical comments can soon have a negative effect.
2. Non-verbal communication – a large majority of communication is achieved through non-verbal means. Non-verbal communication can include the use of body language, gestures, hand signals, facial expressions, volume and tone of voice. In a sporting environment where it is often difficult to hear, we may need to use non-verbal communication a lot.
3. Listening – listening is not just hearing the other person. It is important to acknowledge and understand what they are saying. Good leaders will listen to their group when it is appropriate.
4. Demonstrating – demonstrations help participants learn new skills by showing them the way it should be done. It is important to make sure the demonstration is kept simple and uses the correct technique so that bad habits are not copied.

Organisation of equipment

Sports leaders will use a variety of equipment and resources when delivering their sessions. It is important to consider what equipment and facilities you will need and have available for the specific session you are running. When planning your use of equipment you need to consider whom you are leading, where it is taking place, how many participants you have and any special considerations such as health and safety. When the session is complete you must make sure that the equipment is returned in safe, working condition.

Figure 1.3 Sports leaders should ensure they have the appropriate equipment

Knowledge

A good sports leader will have knowledge of many areas and this develops with experience over time. Sports leaders will have a good knowledge of health and safety issues and know how to complete risk assessments in order to ensure the safety of their participants. They should also know about normal and emergency operating procedures for the facilities they are using.

Sports leaders will need to have good knowledge of the sports and activities they are leading. This would include knowledge of the skills, techniques, rules and tactics of the sport itself. If the sport requires specialist equipment then the leader must know how to use and demonstrate the equipment.

It is also important that the leader has a good knowledge of the participants. Each participant has individual needs and having a good knowledge of this will enable the leader to plan better activities and to address specific issues such as injury, illness or learning difficulties.

Each sport has certain specific fitness requirements and it is therefore essential that the leader has knowledge of the components of fitness that are required in the sports they are leading. This is so that the participants develop sport-specific fitness.

Advanced skills

Activity structure

When planning sessions good leaders will be aware of how to use the time effectively, maximise learning and ensure health and safety. Each of these elements will influence the structure of the activities. The leader must ensure fast transition between different parts of the session using clear and simple instructions, and that the activities themselves match the aims of the session. They should also ensure that the drills and practices are organised in such a way that they reduce the risk of harm to the participants. The activities should not be too complicated as this can lead to injury, loss of interest and confusion on the part of the participants.

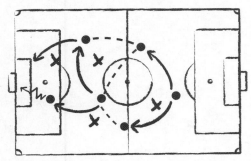

Figure 1.4 The activity should have a structure

Target setting

It is important that sports leaders set targets for their participants to see how they are progressing and to maintain motivation. Targets can be set relating to many different areas, such as the improvement of fitness, learning new techniques or improving knowledge of rules or tactics. Leaders should have clear targets for the things they want the participants to learn from the session and these should contribute to longer term targets.

- Short-term – set over a short period of time, between one day (session) and one month
- Medium-term – these fill the gap between short and long-term targets and should give progressive support towards achievement of the long-term target
- Long-term – these targets relate to longer periods, such as 6–12 months or longer. Most long-term targets are set over the course of a year or 'season'.

These are only guidelines and the timeframes may be longer or shorter depending on different circumstances.

Use of language

The use of language can play a key role in communication. The language should be appropriate for your audience, for example, you would speak to a group of five-year-olds differently from how you would speak to a group of adults. It is important that you do not use technical jargon that may confuse the participants. Your language should be positive to encourage and motivate your participants and it is essential that you use clean language, particularly when leading children.

Figure 1.5 Leaders must ensure they communicate in a way that is appropriate to their audience

Evaluation

A good sports leader will take time to evaluate his or her own performance as well as that of the participants. Evaluating participants will allow the leader to plan the next session to suit their development needs. Self-evaluation will allow the leader to identify what worked well and what did not, and how the session can be made more enjoyable. The leader should use feedback from the participants rather than relying on their own ideas and opinions.

Qualities

Studied

Appearance

The sports leader sets a standard to the participants that they lead and therefore they should have good personal hygiene and dress appropriately at all times, for example, being washed, using deodorant and dressing in sport appropriate clothing. Many participants see the leader as a role model and by presenting yourself in an appropriate way you will gain the respect of the group. When adopting these standards you will also find that you are more confident when delivering sessions.

Enthusiasm

Leaders set the tone for the session and as such should make sure they demonstrate enthusiasm throughout. The language should be positive, they should encourage and motivate and show genuine passion for their sport. Keeping the session going at a good pace will keep the participants active and keen. A leader who is not enthusiastic will find that their sessions are not enjoyable; the participants may become bored and may decide not to come to further sessions. A good sports leader needs to be optimistic when things look glum.

Figure 1.6 Leaders set the tone

Confidence

A confident leader will make fewer mistakes, become less frustrated and maintain focus. Mistakes are unavoidable but a confident leader deals with them and learns from them. A self-assured leader will also find that the participants are also more confident and have more trust in them. A display of confidence also shows the group that the leader is capable and competent in leading activities.

Additional qualities

Studied

Leadership style

Leaders will vary their leadership style depending on whom and what they are leading. The following leadership styles are commonly used in sport:

- Autocratic – this style of leadership is strict. It does not consider the views of the group; neither does it allow individuals to choose their own way of getting the job done. This type of leadership is most effective where there is a risk or certain rules have to be followed.
- Democratic – this style of leadership considers the individual views of group members. The group members have more say but the final decision rests with the leader.
- Laissez-faire – this particular style believes in non-intervention. The group makes all the decisions. This is useful for a highly motivated group or one that has excellent knowledge and skills.

Motivation

Good sports leaders are self-motivated and work for their own sense of achievement and satisfaction; this is called intrinsic motivation. Leaders may also be extrinsically motivated by money or prizes. Good motivation will enable the leader to plan effectively, ensure good organisation and deliver fun and exciting sessions.

Figure 1.7 Medals and prizes may motivate some leaders

Humour

Good humour on the part of the leader will make sessions more fun for the participants. Humour can also promote creativity and encourage a more playful atmosphere. Humour is often used to break up boring or difficult routines or to allow the participants to cope with demanding training sessions. Humour must be used at the appropriate times otherwise it can have a negative impact.

Figure 1.8 Good humour makes the session fun

Personality

Personality means all the traits and characteristics that make up a person and can be seen as a combination of the qualities already covered. Leaders will have a range of different personality traits, some of which are well suited to sports leadership, such as empathy.

Leaders should also know the personalities of their participants. Understanding this will allow the leader to know what motivates different people, how they learn and who they form relationships with in the group.

Topic A.3 Responsibilities

Core responsibilities

Professional conduct

The leader should behave appropriately at all times. Professional conduct means having the correct qualifications and experience, dressing appropriately, respecting all athletes, officials and opponents, promoting fair play and honesty and using suitable language at all times.

Figure 1.9 Sports leaders should promote fair play and honesty

Health and safety

The sports leader is responsible for the health and safety of all participants. The leader will conduct risk assessments, and ensure that equipment is safe and working correctly to reduce the risk of any potential injuries. They should know emergency procedures for the facilities they are working in and ensure the rules and regulations of the sport they are leading are applied fairly and consistently.

Equality

The Equality Act 2010 makes it illegal to discriminate against anyone based on certain beliefs, attitudes or characteristics. A good leader will ensure that equal opportunities are given to all participants without prejudice. The leader must make sure that their sessions are accessible to all and that considerations about gender, race, disability and so on are made on a person to person basis.

Figure 1.10 It is illegal to discriminate on the grounds of age, sex, disability or race

Wider responsibilities

Studied ▢

Insurance

Leaders are required to have appropriate insurance cover to participate in and lead sports activities. If someone is injured in the session then the leader may be deemed to be liable and could be considered negligent as it is the responsibility of the leader to ensure the safety of all. An insurance policy is protection for the leader in case something does go wrong.

Child protection

Child protection is a major issue in sports leadership due to some high profile examples of where children have been abused in the care of sports leaders. Group leaders should not put their participants at risk and should be trained to spot the potential signs of abuse. They should ensure that children can enjoy their activities while in a safe environment. All sports leaders must now undergo a criminal records bureau (CRB) check to ensure they are safe to work with children.

Figure 1.11 Leaders need a CRB check before working with children

Legal obligations

Sports leaders have a legal duty of care for the health and safety of others who may be affected by their actions. You are said to have a duty of care when it is 'reasonably foreseeable' that your actions may cause harm. Duty of care is said to be breached when the standard of care falls short of the 'accepted standard'. In this case the leader may be considered negligent and can be held liable.

There are also a number of legal acts that have been passed by the UK government that are designed to ensure the health and safety of young people:the Children Act (1989), the Protection of Children Act (1999) and the Care Standards Act (2000). It is important that the sports leader is aware of these laws and that they take steps to ensure compliance with them. The NSPCC has published standards for safeguarding and protecting children in sport. These documents will be useful in understanding the different requirements as they are based on good practice, legislation and research, and can be downloaded from www.nspcc.org.uk.

Ethics and values

Ethics is a set of principles of correct conduct. Ethical actions are ones that are fair, honest and responsible and it is important for leaders to demonstrate these to their participants.

Values are thoughts and ideas we believe are important. In sport, this would include fair play, mutual respect and sportsmanship. The leader should discourage any antisocial behaviour.

Rules and regulations

A good sports leader must demonstrate a good knowledge of the rules and regulations of the sport they are leading. They should pass this knowledge on to their participants and be a good role model to the athletes. Sound application of the rules and laws will also help to reduce the risk of injury to the participants and promote fair play and sportsmanship.

Successful sports leaders

Studied

You should be able to recognise these skills, qualities and responsibilities in the variety of sports leaders you have come across when participating in sports activities. Your sports leaders may not display all of these attributes and some will have strengths and weaknesses in particular areas. All sports leaders use their own unique set of attributes to produce effective sports sessions.

Knowledge recap

1. Give examples of the types of sports leaders we find in the sport and leisure industry.

2. Identify the main skills and qualities associated with good sports leaders.

3. Identify the main responsibilities required of good sports leaders.

Assessment guidance for learning aim A

Scenario

You have been asked to attend an interview by the local council for the role of sports leader for the summer holidays. As part of the interview process you have been asked to complete a report on the skills, qualities and responsibilities of sports leaders which you will present at interview.

(2A.P1) **Describe, using relevant examples, the attributes required for, and responsibilities of, sports leadership**

Assessor report: The command word in this criterion is **describe**. This means you have to give the key features and characteristics of the attributes and responsibilities of sports leadership.

✍️ Learner answer

Sports leaders have to have a wide range of skills and qualities in order to be effective when leading sports activity sessions. There are also a number of responsibilities that the leader needs to be aware of and deal with in the planning process.

A sports leader needs to be a good communicator. Communication can come in different forms, for example it can be verbal or non-verbal. Verbal communication should be clear and use language that the participants can understand. Non-verbal communication is the use of gestures, facial expressions and body language and can be used in sport where verbal communication is difficult e.g. when the crowd is too noisy. Listening is also an important part of communication and good leaders will listen to their participants, especially when they have good ideas e.g. new set piece moves. Demonstrations can also be used by leaders to show the participants how to do a skill e.g. showing how to hold a cricket bat properly.

Organisation of sports equipment is an important skill for sports leaders. They must make sure they have enough working equipment to cater for the number of participants they have in the session. Leaders will also need to check that the equipment is safe to use e.g. climbing ropes are not frayed, to ensure health and safety. The equipment should be returned and stored safely for the next user.

Having a good knowledge of the rules, skills, techniques and tactics of the activity is another important skill. The leader will need to use this knowledge to plan effective sessions and make sure they are teaching the participants correctly. A leader should know something about the participants, for example, medical conditions and know about the health and safety aspects of the activity they are leading.

Activity session should have clear goals. Good leaders will set SMARTER goals for what they want to achieve from the session. Goals should be specific, measurable, achievable, realistic, time-related, exciting and recorded. Long-term goals should be set as the end result of the plan with short and medium goals which help as stepping stones to the long-term target. For example, the long-term goal may be to learn how to play a forward defensive shot in cricket but the short-term goal would be to learn how to hold the bat first.

Effective leaders will always try and improve their performance and that of the participants. They should evaluate the strengths and weaknesses of their sessions and set targets for their improvement to build on their weaknesses. Evaluating the performers will help the leader to plan for future sessions e.g. if the participants have not fully learned the skill it can be covered again in the next session.

Sports leaders will show confidence, enthusiasm and their appearance should be professional. Confidence is the belief in your own ability and confident leaders gain the respect of their participants and bounce back from mistakes well. Enthusiasm is interest in what you are doing and showing passion helps to make sessions fun for the participants e.g. staying positive, smiling and showing genuine interest. Leaders will also be dressed appropriately and have good personal hygiene e.g. having the correct kit.

Leaders should be aware that different activities and groups may need different leadership styles. For example, a dangerous activity or difficult group may need a more autocratic approach where the decisions are made solely by the leader. In general a more democratic approach is taken where the opinions of the participants are heard and considered before the leader makes the final decision. Finally a highly skilled or self-motivated group may benefit from a laissez-faire approach where the participants are left to make their own decisions.

Self-motivation is a good quality to have in a sports leader. This means that they get things done without being asked by others. This is called intrinsic motivation and comes from within the individual e.g. enjoyment. Leaders can also be motivated by external rewards e.g. prizes, this is called extrinsic motivation.

Personality means all the traits that make up a person. A leader will need to know the personalities of their participants to be able to prepare for individual needs. The leader themselves will have to show positive personality traits like confidence, enthusiasm and humour. Humour is the ability to see something as funny and it is important in a leader to keep sessions fun and interesting.

The responsibilities of a leader are many. The leader should uphold ethical principles. This means behaving to accepted standards. For example, showing professional conduct by respecting others at all times, promoting fair play and honesty and demonstrating a good knowledge of the rules which is passed on to others. The values of sportsmanship and fair play should also be promoted to participants.

There are legal obligations that the leader should be aware of. There are a number of pieces of legislation that the leader needs to consider. Leaders should also have a CRB check to make sure they are safe to work with children. There are also legal duties to do with equality.

Finally, the leader needs to pay full attention to health and safety. Leaders should do risk assessments of the activities that they have planned and get informed consent from the participants. This is where the participants are told exactly what is contained the plan and that they have agreed to participate. If there is a failure in health and safety, the leader may be held responsible for the harm that comes to participants and therefore it is also important that the leader has insurance e.g. public liability insurance covers you for the injury or death of anyone who is under your care, should you be found liable for the incident.

Assessor report: The report provides some good descriptions of the attributes of successful leaders. There are multiple examples that help to clarify the key points. Many of the skills, qualities and responsibilities given in the unit content are described.

Assessor report – overall

What is good about this assessment evidence?

The report is very detailed and covers a wide range of attributes and responsibilities of sport leaders. The examples provided illustrate the descriptions well and add to the learner's understanding of the topic.

What could be improved in this assessment evidence?

Some of the attributes described in the unit specification are not included in the answer. The learner would need to add in a description of the importance of activity structure and the use of language, with examples of how these would help to improve the success of the leader. The learner has also not provided examples of legal obligations and equal opportunities to add to the description provided.

For the merit criterion there should be reasons to explain how or why the attributes and responsibilities are important when related to leading sports activity sessions.

(2A.M1) Explain the attributes required for, and responsibilities of, sports leadership

Assessor report: The command verb in the criterion is **explain**. This means you have to say how or why each of the skills, qualities and responsibilities is important when planning sports activity sessions.

✍ Learner answer

Sports leaders have to have a wide range of skills and qualities in order to be effective when leading sports activity sessions. There are also a number of responsibilities that the leader needs to be aware of and deal with in the planning process.

A sports leader needs to be a good communicator. Communication can come in different forms, for example it can be verbal or non-verbal. Verbal communication should be clear and use language that the participants can understand. Non-verbal communication is the use of gestures, facial expressions and body language and can be used in sport where verbal communication is difficult e.g. when the crowd is too noisy. Listening is also an important part of communication and good leaders will listen to their participants, especially when they have good ideas e.g. new set piece moves. Demonstrations can also be used by leaders to show the participants how to do a skill e.g. showing how to hold a cricket bat properly. Good communication is important because it means that the participants have a better understanding of what to do in the session, which means they will be on task more and are more likely to achieve the session goals. Demonstrations can be important because a picture paints a thousand words. A simple demonstration can be seen and copied by the participant whereas a long verbal description may be lost on them. This means they are more likely to do the skill well **(a)**.

Organisation of sports equipment is an important skill for sports leaders. They must make sure they have enough working equipment to cater for the number of participants they have in the session. Leaders will also need to check that the equipment is safe to use e.g. climbing ropes are not frayed, to ensure health and safety. The equipment should be returned and stored safely for the next user.

Having a good knowledge of the rules, skills, techniques and tactics of the activity is another important skill. The leader will need to use this knowledge to plan effective sessions and make sure they are teaching the participants correctly. A leader should know something about the participants, for example, medical conditions and know about the health and safety aspects of the activity they are leading. A good knowledge of the sport, the participants and planning is important because it will ensure that the individual needs of the participants are met. It will also help to ensure that the participants are progressing because the skills are being taught correctly. Safe planning will also ensure that the risk of injury to the participants is reduced; for example, if a medical condition is known then the leader can take steps to make sure that if anything unfortunate happens they can deal with it effectively **(a)**.

Activity session should have clear goals. Good leaders will set SMARTER goals for what they want to achieve from the session. Goals should be specific, measurable, achievable, realistic, time-related, exciting and recorded. Long-term goals should be set as the end result of the plan with short and medium goals which help as stepping stones to the long-term target. For example, the long-term goal may be to learn how to play a forward defensive shot in cricket but the short-term goal would be to learn how to hold the bat first. Setting goals increases the chances of successful results. Goals are motivating if they are set correctly and keep the participant interested and determined. Setting short and medium-term goals help to maintain motivation because achieving small successes help make the long-term goal more achievable **(a)**.

Effective leaders will always try and improve their performance and that of the participants. They should evaluate the strengths and weaknesses of their sessions and set targets for their improvement to build on their weaknesses. Evaluating the performers will help the leader to plan for future sessions e.g. if the participants have not fully learned the skill it can be covered again in the next session. Good evaluation is important because it allows continual improvement of both the leader and the participants. This means that new skills are learnt. The leader can also see what worked well, what did not and the reasons why so that planning can be improved in the future **(a)**.

Sports leaders will show confidence and enthusiasm, and their appearance should be professional. Confidence is the belief in your own ability, and confident leaders gain the respect of their participants and bounce back from mistakes well. Enthusiasm is interest in what you are doing and showing passion helps to make sessions fun for the participants e.g. staying positive, smiling and showing genuine interest. Leaders will also be dressed appropriately and have good personal hygiene e.g. having the correct kit. Showing a good appearance gains respect from others and helps set a good example for the participants. Confidence is important because mistakes are bound to happen and you have to be able to get over them and learn from them so that the session is better next time. Good enthusiasm is important because it helps to maintain motivation, makes you more approachable and keeps the session enjoyable **(a)**.

Leaders should be aware that different activities and groups may need different leadership styles. For example, a dangerous activity or difficult group may need a more autocratic approach where the decisions are made solely by the leader. In general a more democratic approach is taken where the opinions of the participants are heard and considered before the leader makes the final decision. Finally a highly skilled or self-motivated group may benefit from a laissez-faire approach where the participants are left to make their own decisions.

Self-motivation is a good quality to have in a sports leader. This means that they get things done without being asked by others. This is called intrinsic motivation and comes from within the individual e.g. enjoyment. Leaders can also be motivated by external rewards e.g. prizes, which is called extrinsic motivation. Having good motivation is important in a leader because a lot of the time leaders are left to their own devices, and without motivation the planning and organisation of sessions may be poor which makes the sessions less enjoyable, more dangerous and less likely to achieve the aims **(a)**.

Personality means all the traits that make up a person. A leader will need to know the personalities of their participants to be able to prepare for individual needs. The leader themselves will have to show positive personality traits like confidence, enthusiasm and humour. Humour is the ability to see something as funny and it is important in a leader to keep sessions fun and interesting. Good humour is important because the sessions are more likely to be fun which keeps people coming back. Understanding the personality of others means that you know what motivates them, what they enjoy and what they dislike so that the session plan can be suited to individual needs **(a)**.

The responsibilities of a leader are many. The leader should uphold ethical principles. This means behaving to accepted standards. For example, showing professional conduct by respecting others at all times, promoting fair play and honesty and demonstrating a good knowledge of the rules which is passed on to others. The values of sportsmanship and fair play should also be promoted to participants. Each of these elements is important because you are being a good role model. Your behaviour is likely to be copied by your participants so it is important to set a good example. Showing good sportsmanship and abiding by the rules will also reduce the chance that someone will get injured **(a)**.

There are legal obligations that the leader should be aware of. There are a number of pieces of legislation that the leader needs to consider. Leaders should also have a CRB check to make sure they are safe to work with children. There are also legal duties to do with equality.

Finally, the leader needs to pay full attention to health and safety. Leaders should do risk assessments of the activities that they have planned and get informed consent from the participants. This is where the participants are told exactly what is contained the plan and have agreed to participate. If there is a failure in health and safety, the leader may be held responsible for the harm that comes to participants and therefore it is also important that the leader has insurance e.g. public liability insurance covers you for the injury or death of anyone who is under your care, should you be found liable for the incident. Insurance is important because you can be sued for a lot of money if you are found to be negligent. Risk assessment is important because it allows you to identify risks and hazards related to the activity and take action to reduce the risk, thereby reducing the risk of harm to your participants **(a)**.

Assessor report: After describing the key attributes and responsibilities the learner has provided an explanation of why they are important for sports leaders **(a)**. The explanations are clearly linked to the attribute or responsibility described.

Assessor report – overall

What is good about this assessment evidence?

The learner has explained the attributes and responsibilities as they have been described. This is good as the assessor can easily see that the attributes and responsibilities have been explained and it makes assessment easier. If any information was missing it can be easily fed back to the learner.

What could be improved in this assessment evidence?

The information that was missing in the pass answer is still missing, that is, activity structure, language and the examples for legal obligations and equal opportunities. In addition to this, you can see that for 'organisation of equipment' there is no highlighted (a) after the description, indicating that there is no explanation for this attribute. The same is true of the importance of leadership style. To achieve M1 the learner must include the descriptions and explanations of all the attributes and responsibilities given in the unit content.

If you are combining the pass and merit response it may be worthwhile using your examples to contribute to the explanation of each attribute and responsibility to clearly show why they are important in the context of the example.

Describe the attributes of two selected successful sports leaders

Assessor report: The command verb in this criterion is **describe**. This means that you have to give the key features and characteristics of two selected sports leaders. The leaders do not have to be famous.

✍ Learner answer

I am going to describe the key attributes of two sports leaders that I know; the first is Mr Smith who is my P.E. teacher and the second is Mrs Smith who is my hockey coach.

Mr Smith is very good at organising the equipment. He always makes sure there is enough for everyone in the group and checks that it is safe to use before every session. He is always dressed appropriately and has excellent knowledge of the rules, techniques and tactics of the sports that we are playing.

Mr Smith uses the autocratic approach most of the time in his lessons and he hardly ever has a laugh in lessons. He also does not seem very enthusiastic when he teaches us and sometimes shouts at us to get things done. He often uses some language that some of us are not familiar with when talking about the technical parts of the game. This is helped by the fact that he demonstrates the things he wants us to do.

The activities we do in class are always well planned and we move from activity to activity without any fuss. The skills we practice always follow on from each other and increase in difficulty as we go through the lesson.

Mrs Smith is an excellent communicator. She always puts things in terms we understand and uses demonstrations to show us exactly what to do. She is always really enthusiastic and always has a smile on her face. She is really funny and never boring and she is always joking around with us.

She does have an excellent knowledge of hockey as she is a qualified umpire and played at county level when she was younger.

Mrs Smith always takes pride in her appearance and wears her county hockey kit to all training sessions. She might forget some equipment at times but always makes sure we have the correct safety equipment or she does not let us play.

Assessor report: The learner has described the attributes of two sports leaders. The learner comments on a range of attributes and describes what the two leaders are good at and what they are not so good at.

Assessor report – overall

What is good about this assessment evidence?

The learner uses two leaders that they are familiar with. This enables the learner to describe their attributes well because they know the leaders personally.

What could be improved in this assessment evidence?

Mrs Smith's negative attributes have not been considered and the learner would need to provide the same level of detail for Mrs Smith as they have done for Mr Smith, covering her leadership style, organisation and motivation.

The learner needs to clearly indicate what impact these attributes will have on the learner to achieve the merit criterion.

Evaluate the attributes of two successful sports leaders

Assessor report: The command verb in this criterion is **evaluate**. This means that you have to say how their attributes will impact on their participants.

✍ Learner answer

I am going to describe and evaluate the key attributes of two sports leaders that I know; the first is Mr Smith who is my P.E. teacher and the second is Mrs Smith who is my hockey coach.

Mr Smith is very good at organising the equipment. He always makes sure there is enough for everyone in the group and checks that it is safe to use before every session. This is good because it means that everyone can take part in the session and get plenty of practice of the skills he is teaching us. He checks to see if it is safe so that we do not get injured through faulty equipment **(a)**. He is always dressed appropriately and has excellent knowledge of the rules, techniques and tactics of the sports that we are playing. The fact that his appearance is always appropriate means he gets the respect of the class and sets a good example for us all to copy **(a)**.

Mr Smith uses the autocratic approach most of the time in his lessons and he hardly ever has a laugh in lessons, which makes his sessions a bit dull and boring. Mr Smith's leadership style is good for some activities e.g. when he is teaching us a new skill. He takes control and helps us to stay safe and learn the basic skills quickly but most of the time he does not listen to our ideas and this sometimes makes us feel discouraged **(a)**. He also does not seem very enthusiastic when he teaches us and sometimes shouts at us to get things done. He often uses some language that some of us are not familiar with when talking about the technical parts of the game. This is helped by the fact that he demonstrates the things he wants us to do so it usually becomes clear and we can see exactly what techniques we are expected to use. This means that we can still learn new skills **(a)**.

The activities we do in class are always well planned and we move from activity to activity without any fuss. The skills we practice always follow on from each other and increase in difficulty as we go through the lesson. This is good because we are always being challenged. There is never any messing about in his lessons which means we have more time to spend on developing our skills (a).

Mrs Smith is an excellent communicator. She always puts things in terms we understand and uses demonstrations to show us exactly what to do. This means we know exactly what to do and can copy her technique which is always good (a). She is always really enthusiastic and always has a smile on her face. She is really funny and never boring and she is always joking around with us.

Mrs Smith is more like a friend and she lets us do whatever we want in the sessions. I would say she has a laissez-faire leadership style. This is not always the best because we mess about a lot and we don't always work on the things we need to in training. Her sessions seem a bit disorganised e.g. we go from shooting to passing and back to shooting again in one session. She also sometimes turns up without the right equipment for the session. One time she did not bring any bibs and it was difficult to know who was on whose team. Her lack of organisation in planning and in the sessions means that we are not improving as fast as we could be. The lack of structure in the session means that a lot of time is wasted and it is difficult to see how the skills we are practising link together and are related to the game and our individual needs (a). She does have an excellent knowledge of hockey as she is a qualified umpire and played at county level when she was younger. Her excellent knowledge means that we always use the correct techniques and we are developing our knowledge of hockey (a).

Mrs Smith always takes pride in her appearance and wears her county hockey kit to all training sessions. This inspires us because we all want to play county hockey and we can see that it is possible. She is also being a good role model by showing us how we should present ourselves (a). She might forget some equipment at times but always makes sure we have the correct safety equipment or she does not let us play.

Assessor report: The learner has taken many of the attributes for the two leaders and evaluated the impact they would have on the participant **(a)** by saying what it is about the attributes that leads to their success as sports leaders.

Assessor report – overall

What is good about this assessment evidence?

The work follows the same structure of the pass work and evaluates the impact of the personal attributes of the two leaders as they are described. This helps to ensure that all attributes are evaluated and none are missed out.

What could be improved in this assessment evidence?

You can see from the answer that not all of the descriptions are followed by an evaluation (there is no **(a)**). In order to achieve the merit criterion the learner would need to evaluate the attributes of knowledge and communication for Mr Smith and the impact of enjoyment, enthusiasm and safety on the participants for Mrs Smith.

2A.D1 Compare and contrast the attributes of two successful sports leaders

Assessor report: The command verbs in this criterion are **compare** and **contrast**. This means you have to say what is different and what the similarities are between the two leaders.

📣 Learner answer

Similarities

Attribute	Mr Smith	Mrs Smith
Knowledge	He has excellent knowledge of the rules, techniques and tactics of the sports that we are playing. His excellent knowledge also means that we are using the correct techniques and we are developing our knowledge of the sports we do.	She does have an excellent knowledge of hockey as she is a qualified umpire and played at county level when she was younger. Her excellent knowledge means that we always use the correct techniques and we are developing our knowledge of hockey.
Appearance		Mrs Smith always takes pride in her appearance and wears her county hockey kit to all training sessions. This inspires us because we all want to play county hockey and we can see that it is possible. She is also being a good role model by showing us how we should present ourselves.
Demonstrations	This is helped by the fact that he demonstrates the things he wants us to do so it usually becomes clear and we can see exactly what techniques we are expected to use. This means that we can still learn new skills.	

Differences

Attribute	Mr Smith	Mrs Smith
Communication	He often uses some language that some of us are not familiar with when talking about the technical parts of the game. His communication is not always the best because it can make us feel like we are useless and the words he uses mean we do not always know what to do.	Mrs Smith is an excellent communicator. She always puts things in terms we understand and uses demonstrations to show us exactly what to do. This means we know exactly what to do and can copy her technique which is always good.
Organisation/Structure	Mr Smith is very good at organising the equipment. He always makes sure there is enough for everyone in the group and checks that it is safe to use before every session. This is good because it means that everyone can take part in the session and get plenty of practice of the skills he is teaching us. He checks to see if it is safe so that we do not get injured through faulty equipment.	Her sessions seem a bit disorganised e.g. we go from shooting to passing and back to shooting again in one session. She also sometimes turns up without the right equipment for the session. One time she did not bring any bibs and it was difficult to know who was on whose team. Her lack of organisation in planning and in the sessions means that we are not improving as fast as we could be. The lack of structure in the session means that a lot of time is wasted and it is difficult to see how the skills we are practising link together and are related to the game and our individual needs.

Learning aim A: Know the attributes associated with successful sports leaders

Attribute	Mr Smith	Mrs Smith
Humour		She always has a smile on her face. She is really funny and never boring and she is always joking around with us. This makes her sessions really enjoyable and I always look forward to training. Her enthusiasm really comes across and she inspires and motivates me to play hockey.
Enthusiasm	He also does not seem very enthusiastic when he teaches us and sometimes shouts at us to get things done. He often uses some language that some of us are not familiar with when talking about the technical parts of the game. His communication is not always the best because it can make us feel like we are useless and the words he uses mean we do not always know what to do.	She is always really enthusiastic and always has a smile on her face. She is really funny and never boring and she is always joking around with us. This makes her sessions really enjoyable and I always look forward to training. Her enthusiasm really comes across and she inspires and motivates me to play hockey.
Leadership style	Mr Smith uses the autocratic approach most of the time in his lessons and he hardly ever has a laugh in lessons. Mr Smith's leadership style is good for some activities e.g. when he is teaching us a new skill. He takes control and helps us to stay safe and learn the basic skills quickly but most of the time he does not listen to our ideas and this sometimes makes us feel discouraged.	

Assessor report: The learner has shown how the two leaders are similar and different in some of the attributes that were discussed in the pass and merit criteria.

Assessor report – overall

What is good about this assessment evidence?

As you can see the information contained in the tables is the same as the merit work which means that this format reduces your workload. If it is set out in this format you will automatically achieve the D1 criterion as long as the evidence towards P2 and M2 meets the grading criteria.

What could be improved in this assessment evidence?

The table shows a good way of comparing and contrasting the two leaders but to achieve D1 the learner would need to complete the missing cells in the table, that is, show the similarities and differences for all attributes listed.

The evidence could be further enhanced by providing more specific examples to illustrate the similarities and differences between the two leaders.

Learning aim B
Undertake the planning and leading of sports activities

Assessment criteria

2B.P3   Plan two selected sports activities.

2B.M3   Justify the choice of activities within the sports activity plan.

2B.P4   Independently lead a sports activity session.

2B.M4   Lead a successful sports activity session.

Topic B.1 Sports activities

Planning a session

Studied ☐

Planning a sports activity means that you will have to look at every detail and consider every eventuality. The time spent planning may be time-consuming but it will help ensure that you get the most out of your sessions.

The first thing to consider is: what is the activity that you wish to carry out? Sessions could include:

- A team sport, such as football, rugby, netball, hockey, cricket
- An individual sport, such as badminton, squash, golf, athletics, swimming
- A fitness session such as circuit, weights session, flexibility.

Topic B.2 Components of sports activity session

Different sessions will have different requirements and plans should be tailored to specific needs. A typical session will contain the following:

Warm up

Studied ☐

A warm up is typically made up of three elements: a pulse-raising activity, some mobility and flexibility exercises and sports-specific skills that help prepare the participant for the activities in the session. It is important to make sure that the skill-related activities in the warm up are related in some way to the planned activities, for example, a game of tag rugby would be a good warm up for a session that focuses on passing and receiving the ball.

Main component

Studied ☐

Depending on the type and the aims of the session the main component can vary. For a fitness session the main component would be fitness work. The main aim would be to focus on one or two components of fitness and work on that using an accepted method of fitness training such as circuit training, interval training or resistance work.

When leading sport-related activities the main component may include some or all of the following:

- Skill introduction – whatever the main aims of the session are, this element is designed to introduce the skill. It may involve a simple drill where the basic technique is practised in a fixed or artificial situation, for example, passing a stationary ball to a partner.
- Development – as the session progresses the drills should become more and more challenging in order to make the practise more game-specific. The development of these skills is called 'progression'. Progressions are achieved by bringing in more complex situations, for example, passing a moving ball or passing to keep the ball away from an opponent.
- Conditioned game – a conditioned game is designed to reinforce the elements that were practised in the drills. A conditioned game will have certain rules that help the participants put into practise the skills they have developed in the session so far, for example, one touch passing.
- Final activity – the final activity could be an unconditioned game or it may be used to practise other elements, such as tactical play or set pieces.

Cool down

Studied ☐

The main aim of the cool down is to promote recovery and to return the body to pre-training levels. The cool down should include an activity that slowly reduces the heart rate, for example, a slow jog to a walk. This is also an ideal opportunity to introduce some flexibility work as the muscles are at their most flexible at the end of the session.

Learning aim B: Undertake the planning and leading of sports activities

Topic B.3 Plan

Proper planning prevents poor performance. Consideration of some key factors will help to make sure that the session runs smoothly and ensures the health and safety of the participants.

Session Planner			
Date:		**Trainer:**	
Activity:		**Duration:**	
Number attending	**M:**	**F:**	**Age range:**
Necessary Equipment:			
Issues to consider (e.g. health issues):			
Session objectives:			

Component	Time	Activity	Notes
Warm up			
Main Activity			
Cool down			
Review (were objectives achieved?):			

Table 2.1 Example of a session plan

Participants

Studied ☐

In order to plan the use of your resources effectively there are certain key bits of information you will need to know about your participants, such as age, ability, gender, numbers, medical issues and specific needs. You will need to ensure that the facilities can cope with the number of people in the session and that you have enough equipment. You will need to match the content of the session to the age and ability of the group so that it is not too easy or too difficult. Identifying medical issues and other individual needs can be done through a health screening questionnaire or PAR Q.

Aims and objectives

Studied

This is what you want to get out of the session. The setting of goals should be done using the SMARTER principle:

Specific – your aims must precise and detailed

Measurable – how can you measure it?

Achievable – it must be possible to achieve the goal

Realistic – be realistic with your aims. Are the goals achievable?

Time-related – set yourself a time period within which to achieve your goal

Exciting – this will help motivate you to achieve your goals

Recorded – record your aims; this will help you stick to them

Resources

Studied

Knowing your resources and how best to use them will allow the leader to get the most out of each session. The equipment must be checked to ensure it is in safe working order and that there is enough to cope with the numbers in the session. Each component of the session should be planned in line with the amount of time there is available. There should also be consideration of the environment in which you will be working, for example, how much space is there? Is it outdoor or indoor? What surface?

Health and safety considerations

Studied

A good leader will evaluate the location for suitability of purpose prior to the activity session. As part of the preparation a risk assessment should be completed. This identifies the risks and hazards associated with the session and takes steps to minimise the risks. It is also a good idea to get the informed consent of the participants prior to the session. Informed consent forms can be found on the internet but they should make clear what the session involves, the potential risks and benefits and have a section filled in by the participant to say they have had all the information and are happy to participate.

Risk Assessment Form – Sport

Regular Activity / Trip or Event * delete where appropriate

NOTTINGHAM TRENT UNIVERSITY
Sports

Sport Club: _____
Activity or Trip/event name: _____
Location: _____
Date & Time: _____
Committee Position & Name: _____

Total score [ ]

Committee Signature: _____
Type name if emailing in

Aimed at: Complete Beginners / Beginners / Intermediate / Advanced / All * delete where appropriate

Score each category e.g. Location, in the box at the top of each column of the table below according to

[ ] [ ] [ ] [ ] [ ] [ ] [ ] [ ]

Score (1 – 5)	Location	Group	Leader(s)	Equipment	Transport	First Aid*	Weather	Activity
1	A managed and staffed centre catering specifically for your activity	Whole group with appropriate competency at and above level of activity	Leaders qualified at or above appropriate level for activity	No equipment or protective clothing required	Activity on site or local, no transport requirements for participants	First Aid available. Access to Emergency support. Persons qualified at appropriate level.	Change in weather will have no adverse effect on group	No physical or strenuous activity (e.g. meal)
2	A managed and staffed centre that is suitable for your activity	Majority of group with appropriate competency at or above level of activity	Leaders experienced in leadership role at or above level of activity	Minimal equipment or protective clothing required to undertake activity. Required for comfort or peace of mind	Use of hired coach or public transport	First Aid not available. Access to Emergency support. Persons qualified at appropriate level.	Change in weather will have minimal effect of activity	Light physical activity no body contact
3	A managed but unstaffed centre or site suitable for your activity	Majority of group with appropriate competency for level of activity with suitable knowledge or supervision	Leaders experienced and competent as a participant at level of activity. No leadership experience at this level	Some equipment or protective clothing required by participants. No training required for use, equipment failure may cause minor injury	Local or regional movement of participants or large/heavy items using self driven vehicles	First Aid available. Access to Emergency Support. No, or insufficient Persons qualified at appropriate level	Change in weather could cause problems if the group is not adequately prepared with training or equipment	Moderate physical activity with medium body contact
4	Unmanaged and unstaffed site or centre suitable for your activity	Group with some competency in activity. Some awareness of risks involved	Leaders with some experience of activity but not at this level. No leadership experience	Complex, delicate or extensive equipment or protective clothing required for some or all participants. Training on use of equipment required. Some reliance on equipment where failure may cause some injury	National movement of participants using self drive vehicles or including over night stay	First Aid not available. No access to Emergency support. Persons qualified at appropriate level	Change in weather could rapidly lead to serious problems if the group is not adequately prepared or equipped	Strenuous physical activity high contact sport
5	A remote location. Unmanaged and unstaffed site	Large proportion of absolute Novices with no or little experience of the activity at any level	No experience of activity as a participant or leader	Complex, delicate or extensive protective clothing required for all participants. Extensive training on use of equipment required. Direct reliance on equipment, failure is likely cause serious injury	Transportation of heavy or large items and many people, use of minibuses and trailers or traveling abroad	First Aid not available. Persons not qualified at appropriate level. With or without access to Emergency support	Change in weather could have very serious repercussions for the group	Involves participants being in or around water 2m or more off the ground

*First Aid - Where are third party is qualified in first aid at an appropriate level, but not a member of an emergency service or your club. e.g. Instructor, attendant at sports facility

Access to Emergency Support - Where trained professionals would be able to be called to an incident within 45 minutes of an incident. e.g. Ambulance, Mountain Rescue, Coast Guard

Persons Qualified - Club members with First Aid Qualification a minimum of 4 hour First Aid Certificate for Societies, Pitch and Racket Sports, 8 hours or more for water sports, outdoor or hazardous activities (specialist certificates may be suitable)

7–11	12–18	19–24	25–29	30–35
Low Risk	Medium Risk	High Risk	Extreme Risk	Unacceptable Risk

Figure 2.1 Risk assessment

Topic B.4 Lead

A sports leader must be able to deliver a session in an effective way. The skills, qualities and responsibilities of good sports leaders have already been described earlier in the unit and all of these must be demonstrated when leading the session.

Figure 2.2 A Successful sports leader needs to demonstrate many skills and qualities

Topic B.5 Measures of success

The success of the session can be determined by assessing how each of the following was achieved:

Coverage of planned components – were all the activities, drills and practices completed? Were the timeframes appropriate? Could the participants do the planned activities? Were the progressions too easy or too hard? Did the session link together well?

Meeting set aims and objectives – to what extent were the session goals achieved? Did all of the participants meet the session goals?

Organisation – were transitions smooth and quick? Did the groupings work well? Was the equipment ready and working? Was everyone on task?

Safety – was a risk assessment completed? Were drills and activities organised to ensure health and safety? Were medical needs considered? Was equipment put away when not in use? Did participants wear the correct clothing and footwear?

Figure 2.3 Measuring success

Knowledge recap

1. What are the components of a warm up?

2. What is the purpose of a cool down?

3. Describe the key factors to consider when planning sports activity sessions.

Learning aim B: Undertake the planning and leading of sports activities

Assessment guidance for learning aim B

Scenario

You have been successful in gaining employment as a sports leader with the local council. As a result you are expected to produce two sports activity session plans that you will use when delivering the sessions to local teenagers. One of these sessions will be delivered and observed by a member of the assessment team to ensure quality of delivery.

(2B.P3) **Plan two selected sports activities**

Assessor report: In order to achieve this criterion you have to create two plans for entire sports sessions (only one of which you will deliver). You must include a warm up, main component and a cool down and record details of the participants, the aims of the session, the resources required and address health and safety issues.

✍ Learner answer

TRAINING PLAN						
Date:	01/09/12	Time:	1pm	Name of coach:	AN Other	
No. of participants:	20			Ability level:	Age:	16
Duration: 1 hour		Location:		Gender:		
Medical Issues:		One participant has asthma, inhaler to be brought to session		Other Issues:	None	
Activity:				Basketball		
Aims of session:						
Risk assessment: Risk assessment complete and informed consent given (please tick and attach) ☑						
Equipment:						

Timings	Session content
10 Mins	Warm up – Follow my leader. Groups of five. Leader dribbles around sports hall and teammates follow and copy the dribbling of the leader. The leader is to use different types of dribble. Change leader every minute (up to five mins). Dynamic stretch of all major muscle groups follow by piggy in the middle. 4v1: four to keep ball from one in limited space. Change every 30 seconds if needed.
30 Mins	Main component –

1. Dribbling up and down the court using right hand, left hand, crossover, between legs, round the back and spin dribble.

2. In pairs, one attacker, one passive defender, use different dribbles to 'beat' the defender. Change regularly.

3. Defender becomes more active and tries to take ball from attacker. Defender can only move side to side. Change regularly.

4. In pairs pass the ball over 10 feet using bounce, chest and overhead pass.

Key: X = cone   ◯ = player   = path of ball

5. Passing square. Five players in each corner. Two balls to start. Player with ball dribbles halfway, passes ahead, follows pass and joins back of group. (Extension – introduce more balls, change direction of pass, change direction of run).

|

10 Mins	Conditioned game – Two games of 5v5 – ten consecutive passes by one team scores two points (no baskets) followed by normal game 5v5 using baskets.
10 Mins	Cool down –

TRAINING PLAN

Date:	02/09/12	Time:	1pm	Name of coach:		AN Other	
No. of participants:				Ability level:	Intermediate	Age:	16
Duration: 1 hour		Location:	Sports hall	Gender:		Mixed	
Medical Issues:		None		Other Issues:		None	
Activity:		Volleyball					

Aims of session:

i) Correctly serve underhand using correct form and get it over the net.

ii) Correctly perform the overhand serve 80% of the time they serve it.

iii) Improve accuracy of passing.

Risk assessment:

Equipment:		20 soft touch volleyballs, 2 volleyball courts
Timings	Session content	
10 Mins	Warm up – Walk into jog – five mins, followed by dynamic stretches of major muscle groups, followed by game of volleyball tag. Person who is 'it' has to tag players with volleyball, no throwing.	
30 Mins	Main component – 1. Volley keep ups. Volley ball to self with one bounce in between advance to no bounce. 2. Volley keep ups with partner with one bounce advance to no bounce. 3. Underarm and overarm throw to partner – ten metres 4. Underarm hit to partner – ten metres 5. Overarm hit to partner – ten metres	

30 Mins	6. Underarm hit to partner with bounce and volley back advance to no bounce.
	7. Overarm hit to partner with bounce and volley back advance to no bounce.
10 Mins	Conditioned game
10 Mins	Cool down- Five mins jogging slowing to walk whilst dribbling, followed by static stretches of major muscles to be held for 20 seconds.

Assessor report: The learner has produced two plans for two different activities. The format of the plans is excellent and there are sections to include information that form the basis for an excellent session plan.

Assessor report – overall

What is good about this assessment evidence?

The plans include some details about the participants, including age, ability, numbers, medical information and gender. The majority of the session content illustrates the components expected of a sports activity session which show progression and match the stated aims.

What could be improved in this assessment evidence?

Certain sections of the session plans have not been included. All details regarding the individuals, equipment, location, ability level, number of participants, the risk assessment and aims should be included in both session plans. In plan 1 there are no details of the cool down activities or intensities, and in plan 2 there is no description of the conditioned game. To achieve a pass the learner must include all of this information.

The learner has not provided a justification of the different elements of the plan. To achieve M3 this must be included.

2B.M3 Justify the choice of activities within the sports activity plan

Assessor report: The command verb in this criterion is **justify**. This means that you have to provide an acceptable reason for including the different elements of the plan.

✍ Learner answer

The participant information is included in the plan so that individual needs can be identified and the plan can be designed to meet those needs. The activities are suited to the age and ability of the participants. The skills are basic to account for the beginners in the basketball plan and are slightly harder for the intermediate ability in the volleyball plan. This enables the intermediate ability players to develop the basic skills they have already learned.

The organisation of the plans allow for quick transition from drill to drill because they change in only one way each time. This means that the participants stay on task for longer and do not become bored with the session. The drills progress throughout the session so that the participants can build on simple skills and practise them in more realistic game-like situations. The organisation of the drills themselves helps to ensure there is less chance of injury because they are done in straight lines so there is less chance that people will run into each other.

The conditioned games are included so that the specific skills that were practised in the main component are practised in a game-specific situation. This helps to put the skills in a game setting so that when the participant is in a game they can show the skills more effectively.

Extension tasks have been provided in both plans. This is so the leader can give the better ability participants more difficult tasks to do when the basic skills are mastered. This will extend those participants and again stop them from becoming bored with tasks that they find too easy. The lower ability participants can be moved on when they are capable but they will not get frustrated by being asked to do things they are not able to do. The development of the skills and their application to game situations are designed to meet the stated aims of the sessions.

Assessor report: The learner has described the majority of the different parts of the plan and provided good reasons for including them. Justification has been provided for a wide range of concepts.

Assessor report – overall

What is good about this assessment evidence?

The learner comments on different parts of the plan and comes up with acceptable reasons for including the various elements. The justification comments on why participant information is included, why the planned activities are included based on ability level and age, and why they have been organised the way they have. There is a clear link between the aims of the plan and how those aims are met.

What could be improved in this assessment evidence?

The learner has not justified the inclusion of the warm up or cool down, and although the learner has mentioned the details of the location and equipment required in the plan, they have not justified the inclusion of these. The learner needs to offer good reasons for the addition of these elements in the plan to achieve M3.

The learner has provided justification of the plans together. There is an opportunity to take each plan in turn and provide a more specific justification for each individual plan.

2B.P4 Independently lead a sports activity session

Assessor report: The command words in this grading criterion are **independently lead**. This means that you have to deliver a sports activity session to a group by yourself without the support of any other individual.

When you are ready to deliver the sports activity session, you should complete the delivery under the direct supervision of an appropriately qualified sports leader while the assessor observes. The session ideally should be visually recorded to ensure that assessment can take place after the event as well and to enable you to carry out your own evaluation of the session. After the session has concluded, the assessor should complete an observation record which clearly details what you did within the session, how you performed, coverage of the unit content, and how you met the requirements of the targeted criteria.

 **Learner answer**

Witness Statement

Learner's name:	AN Other
Qualification:	BTEC First award in sport
Unit number & title:	Unit 6 – Leading sports activities

Description of activity undertaken (please be as specific as possible)
Learner delivered a sports activity session independently using the skills, qualities and attributes of good leaders.

Assessment criteria (to which the activity provides evidence)
2B. P4 Independently lead a sports activity session.
2B. M4 Lead a successful sports activity session.

How the activity meets the requirements of the assessment and grading criteria, including how and where the activity took place
The sports activity session was delivered in the school sports hall in the presence of a qualified sports leader and assessing tutor.
The learner led the session independently, without the help of peers, the sports leader or the tutor.
The learner did not lead a successful session as they did not meet the aims of the session. The session overran on time as the transition from one activity to another was very slow. The organisation of the session was poor, with many participants not knowing what to do.

Witness's name:	J Smith	Job role:	Sports leader	
Witness's signature:			Date:	
Learner's name:	A N Other			
Learner's signature:			Date:	
Assessor's name:	J Jones			
Assessor's signature:			Date:	

Assessor report: By leading the session independently and providing evidence of the session through a witness testimony and video tape the learner has achieved P4.

Assessor report – overall

What is good about this assessment evidence?

The evidence is based on the performance of the individual in leading the sports activity. The fact that it is witnessed and recorded provides other assessors with good evidence that the learner has achieved the criterion.

What could be improved in this assessment evidence?

The assessor has clearly explained why the higher criterion has not been achieved. The learner will need to address these issues to achieve the M4 criterion.

(2B.M4) Lead a successful sports activity session

Assessor report: The key word in this grading criterion is **successful**. In the summary of content the measures of success are described. You need to make sure you have achieved the aims of the session, shown good organisation, ensured health and safety of the participants and covered all the planned aspects of the session.

Learner answer

Witness Statement

Learner's name:	AN Other
Qualification:	BTEC First award in sport
Unit number & title:	Unit 6 – Leading sports activities

Description of activity undertaken (please be as specific as possible)
Learner delivered a sports activity session independently using the skills, qualities and attributes of good leaders.

Assessment criteria (to which the activity provides evidence)
2B. P4 Independently lead a sports activity session.
2B. M4 Lead a successful sports activity session.

How the activity meets the requirements of the assessment and grading criteria, including how and where the activity took place
The sports activity session was delivered in the school sports hall in the presence of a qualified sports leader and assessing tutor.
The learner led the session independently, without the help of peers, the sports leader or the tutor.
The learner led a successful session. All components of the session were delivered with good organisation and equipment was stored safely when not in use. The timings were appropriate and the progressions from activity to activity were smooth and quick. The learner performed a risk assessment before the session and organised the drills to make sure that the likelihood of injury was reduced. The groupings worked well, particularly in the game situation where all participants were on task and performing well. The aims of the session were clearly met by all participants.

Witness's name:	J Smith	Job role:		Sports leader	
Witness's signature:				Date:	
Learner's name:	A N Other				
Learner's signature:				Date:	
Assessor's name:	J Jones				
Assessor's signature:				Date:	

Assessor report: The witness testimony clearly describes how the learner led a successful sports activity session. It clearly states the outcomes in terms of success measures and, with additional video evidence, ensures that the learner has achieved M4.

Assessor report – overall

What is good about this assessment evidence?

The evidence is based on the performance of the individual in leading the sports activity. The fact that it is witnessed and recorded provides other assessors with good evidence of what the learner has done to achieve the criterion.

What could be improved in this assessment evidence?

The quality of this evidence is determined by the quality of the witness statement and the feedback from the assessor. The key is to provide good detail in the feedback to clearly show how the criterion has been met. If recorded, this provides good supporting evidence for the assessor comments and the grade can be verified easily.

Learning aim C
Review the planning and leading of sports activities

Assessment criteria

(2C.P5) Review the planning and leading of the sports activity session, describing strengths and areas for improvement, and targets for future development as a sports leader.

(2C.M5) Explain targets for future development as a sports leader, including a personal development plan.

(2C.D2) Justify targets for future development as a sports leader and activities within the personal development plan.

Topic C.1 Review

Feedback for review

Studied ☐

The review stage of the delivery process is an important opportunity to assess the effectiveness of the session. It is important that you receive feedback from a range of people to make sure you have a range of thoughts and opinions. Feedback should be sought from participants, your supervisor and observers. You should also complete a self-analysis of your performance.

Methods

Studied ☐

The feedback you receive can come in many different forms. Your supervisor or teacher could give a verbal evaluation of your performance at the end of the session. The session could also be recorded so that you can review it at a later time. The benefit of this is that you can look at it again and again if needed.

Figure 3.1 Video analysis

The best way to get feedback off your participants is through a questionnaire or comment cards. The questionnaire should be simple and easy to answer and should cover the main areas on which you would like feedback. This should be prepared before the session and handed to the participants at its completion.

Figure 3.2 Questionnaire

If you are being observed by peers or any other significant individual they could provide you with a copy of their observation records to help you to complete your evaluation.

The feedback you receive should focus on the measures of success previously described, that is, planning and content, achievements, organisation and health and safety. You will also want feedback on how well you have demonstrated the skills, qualities and responsibilities of good leaders that have also been covered earlier in this book.

Strengths

Studied ☐

Using the feedback you should be able to identify the strengths of the session. You should use the information presented in the evaluations to look for positive comments, feelings and opinions. Where there is consistency between the different evaluations, this would suggest that this is a particular area of strength.

Areas for improvement

Studied ☐

You should also be able to use the feedback to identify the areas on which you still need to improve. These factors will support your development and help to plan your targets for future sessions.

Knowledge recap

1. Identify the different ways you can receive feedback from your sports activity sessions.

Topic C.2 Targets for development

After you have completed your review and summarised your strengths and areas of improvement, you need to produce a personal development plan (PDP). This will include targets which you have set for yourself and which address the areas of improvement. The targets you set should use the SMARTER principle. Identifying these targets will help you to improve and deliver effective sports sessions in the future.

Personal development plan			
Name:		**Date:**	
Objectives	**Success criteria**	**Methods**	**Implementation**
What do I want to improve/learn?	How will I measure and review my success/improvement?	How will I achieve my objectives?	How will I put what I've learnt into practice?

Table 3.1 An example of a personal development plan

The development plan should also include other information that is relevant in achieving your targets. This includes:

- **Opportunities** – you should be able to describe what opportunities there are for you to meet your targets. You could meet your targets by achieving better qualifications, or working with other leaders in the community. You could also observe other effective sports leaders who work with specific groups. There is also the option to undertake further training by taking coaching and officiating courses. The development plan should clearly identify the methods which the leader plans to use to improve their performance with a justification of how and why.
- **Possible barriers** – when producing a development plan it is important that a sports leader is aware of the potential barriers to improvement. It is not always possible to implement the development plan due to unforeseen circumstances. It is then up to the sports leader to overcome the issues faced. Potential barriers may include cost, geographical location, time, gender, cultural differences and environment.

Knowledge recap

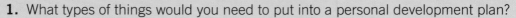

1. What types of things would you need to put into a personal development plan?

2. What barriers to your improvement might you face? Give examples to illustrate your points.

Assessment guidance for learning aim C

Scenario

You have completed the delivery of the session and now you must provide a report on the quality of your sports leading. You should produce a personal development plan to highlight your strengths and areas for improvement, indicating targets for future development.

(2C.P5) **Review the planning and leading of the sports activity session, describing strengths and areas for improvement, and targets for future development as a sports leader**

Assessor report: There are two command words in this criterion. The first is to **review**. This means to look at something critically. The second is to **describe**, which means you need to give the key features and characteristics of something. In this case you need to describe the strengths and areas of improvement of the session and set targets for future improvement of the weaker areas.

✍ Learner answer

The planning of the session went well. I was able to use my knowledge of the sport to plan good drills that were progressed throughout and met the aims of the session. All of the session components were completed and the transitions were quick. This meant the participants were on task for more time and did not have chance to get bored. The planning of the health and safety part of the plan was difficult because I had not done a risk assessment before and I missed a couple of major hazards, however in the end these did not present a problem. In future I will need more training on risk assessment so that I can identify all the potential risks.

At the end of the session I had met the aims. I could see that participants could accurately serve the ball into the court at least 80% of the time and that passing accuracy was better because there were less faults off the serve. This is a real strength because now I can move on to different and more difficult skills.

My enthusiasm and motivation were excellent during the session. The participants said that they enjoyed the session and I think this is because I was smiling, talking and constantly using positive feedback. This is a strength as they were more focused on the task and are more likely to come to another session.

One area I could improve is my use of demonstrations. A few times I did not demonstrate the activity and at first the participants do not quite understand what they had to do. When I did do a demonstration my technique was not the best so some of the participants started to do the incorrect technique until I corrected them. In future I need to use more demonstrations and make sure they are correct. I could also use one of the participants if they can show good technique.

During the final game I found that I was unsure on a few rules, e.g. if the ball is in or out when it hits the line, what to do if the ball hits the net on serve and rules about substitutions. This showed the group a lack of knowledge in this area and as a result my confidence dropped. I need to read up on the rules of volleyball so that I can teach the rules to the participants and apply them in a game.

Assessor report: This evaluation example is based on a fictitious activity session. You should bear in mind that your evaluation should be specific to the session that you delivered and should be informed by the feedback that you get when leading your own activity.

The learner has described areas of strength and improvement for both the planning and leading parts of the session. The strengths are linked to the areas of success that were assessed in learning aim B: covering planned components, meeting aims, organisation and safety as well as other general leadership skills.

Assessor report – overall

What is good about this assessment evidence?

At least three strengths and areas of improvement have been described which shows the learner has considered a range of ideas. There is also reference to the opinion of the participants which shows the learner has used evaluations from others.

What could be improved in this assessment evidence?

The learner has not set SMARTER targets for improvement. To achieve P5, targets should be set that address the specific areas of improvement identified in the main report, for example: to complete a risk assessment training course by 01/10/12. You will see below how this can be achieved through the use of a personal development plan.

2C.M5 Explain targets for future development as a sports leader, including a personal development plan

Assessor report: The command verb in this criterion is **explain**. This means you have to say how or why you have set the targets that you have. The other element to this criterion is to include a personal development plan (PDP). There are numerous PDP templates available online.

✎ Learner answer

Name:	A N Other				
Aim	Short-term goal	Mid-term goal	Long-term goal	What activities do I need to undertake to achieve my aims?	Possible barriers
To complete a risk assessment training course			Attend course and pass by 01/10/12	I need to find a course that meets my needs and is local so that I don't have to travel too far and to keep the costs down. I need to research the area so I can prepare for the course and increase my knowledge and chances of passing. I need to complete the course so that I can spot all the potential hazards and risks when I lead sports activities and my paperwork is accurate.	

Aim	Short-term goal	Mid-term goal	Long-term goal	What activities do I need to undertake to achieve my aims?	Possible barriers
To improve my skills in serving and passing and to use the correct technique	To observe elite players performing the skills	To practise the skills three times per week	To be able to serve and pass accurately 90% of the time	I need to be able to observe elite players so I will use a combination of video analysis and live observation at my local volleyball club. This will enable me to see the correct technique. I will then use the techniques I observed in my own training so that I can improve them and be better prepared to demonstrate them in future.	Lack of video analysis equipment. Poor observation skills. Lack of time to train.
To know the rules about sideouts, serve and substitutions	By next day	By day 5	By next session (day 7)		No officials to follow or no games to be played in time for next session.
Review of targets:					

Assessor report: The learner has produced a PDP template that contains all the required sections expected of a document of this nature. The learner clearly describes some of the strategies that they will adopt and there is some indication of the barriers that the learner could face when attempting to improve.

Assessor report – overall

What is good about this assessment evidence?

The learner has produced a personal development plan that sets out the different areas of development. If each section is filled correctly and with the appropriate detail the merit criterion is targeted well.

What could be improved in this assessment evidence?

To achieve M5, all sections should be complete. The barriers are missing from aim 1 and interim goals should also be set. The targets set for aim 2 are not SMARTER as there is no set date for achievement. In aim 3 there should be stated objectives for each interim goal and a description of the activities that will be done to achieve the improvement.

In order to achieve the distinction criteria the learner needs to justify the targets and activities in the PDP.

Justify targets for future development as a sports leader and activities within the personal development plan

Assessor report: The command verb in this grading criterion is **justify**. This means that you have to provide acceptable reasons for the targets you have set and the activities you intend to do in the PDP.

✍ Learner answer

The short, medium and long-term targets have been set to provide a series of goals that will eventually lead to the improvement of the specific weaknesses that were identified in the review. The breakdown of the goals into smaller targets will help me to achieve the goals in small steps and as I complete each one it will maintain my motivation. The targets have been given a set date so that there is time pressure to meet the deadline. Without this the actions might never be completed. The targets are recorded so that I can keep referring to them and keep on track with the development. All the targets are realistic and attainable which means I will not lose interest in them because they are impossible.

A training course for risk assessment is a good activity to improve my health and safety knowledge because I will learn to spot the hazards and risks that are associated with sports activity sessions. I will also learn how to fill in the risk assessment form accurately to make sure I am meeting the legislation related to health and safety. Knowing how to perform a good risk assessment will ensure that I increase the chances that the participants will stay healthy and safe.

Observation of elite performers is a good way to improve my serving and passing skills because I will be able to see exactly how the technique should be performed. This is followed by regular training which will be a good way to practise the techniques that I have seen.

Reading the official rules of volleyball is the best way to learn the specific rules I am unsure about because there will be no doubt that these are correct. In addition I can make sure that the rules are up to date and I am not teaching my participants old rules. By shadowing an official I can make sure that I have understood the rules and I know how to apply them in a game situation. This means that when I am leading the session again I can teach the participants the correct rules and be consistent and fair in my umpiring of the game.

Assessor report: This evidence should accompany that given for M5 in order to achieve D2. The learner has given good reasons as to why the SMARTER principle has been used to set goals. They have also supported the choice of activities with sound reasons as to how they will improve the learner and benefit the participants.

Assessor report – overall

What is good about this assessment evidence?

The learner has not only justified the targets, they have also justified the activities. The strategies for improvement are also well suited to the achievement of the goals.

What could be improved in this assessment evidence?

The learner has addressed most of the key issues; however they have not stated clearly the benefits of setting measurable and exciting targets. In addition there is no justification of why regular training is an important element of learning new techniques.

The learner could describe other activities that they could do to develop further. For example, to improve the knowledge of the rules the learner could get umpiring qualifications, or to improve their knowledge of demonstrations they could go on a coaching course which would provide them with technical knowledge and effective demonstrations.

Sample assignment brief

PROGRAMME NAME:	BTEC First Award in Sport	
TUTOR NAME:		
STUDENT NAME:		
DATE SET:		SUBMISSION DATE:

This assignment will assess the following learning aims:

A Know the attributes associated with successful sports leaders

B Undertake the planning and leading of sports activities

C Review the planning and leading of sports activities.

Scenario

In preparation for an upcoming employers visit you have been asked to prepare a portfolio of evidence. The employers' group is called Coaches4U and they are looking for potential staff to gain paid work across weekends and in school holidays. Based on your portfolio of evidence for planning, delivery and evaluation they will select a handful of students to be their employees.

Task 1

a) Prepare a Powerpoint presentation that describes the attributes of successful sports leaders. You should also describe the responsibilities required to lead sporting activities successfully.

b) Throughout the slides, explain the attributes and responsibilities associated with successful sports leaders.

c) In the slides describe the attributes of two successful sports leaders (these do not have to be famous sports leaders). Evaluate the strengths and weaknesses of two contrasting sports leaders you have chosen, and say why you think each of them is effective in their roles, relating your examples to the attributes and responsibilities described in task 1a. Make comparisons and contrasts between the sports leaders. State what they have in common and what makes them different from each other even though they both may be successful.

Task 2

a) Choose two sports activities that you would feel competent in delivering to the group.

b) Devise a session plan for one session in each sport including information on participants, equipment, timings, environment, health and safety and session aims. Within this plan should be correct sequencing of the session, progression, coaching points and include warm up, main content and cool down.

c) Give reasons as to why you have chosen the activities within the plan, linking your ideas to the participants, the aims of the session, organisation and health and safety.

d) Lead this session independently, gaining tutor feedback. The success of the session can be measured by how well you cover the planned components, meet the aims and objectives of the session, ensure the safety of the participants and organise the session.

Task 3

Review your own performance as a sports leader in the planning and leading of sports activities. Say what areas you thought you were good at (your strengths) and what areas and factors you feel you need improvement on and further development in, to be a better sports leader.

You need to explain your strengths and areas of improvement, giving suggestions as to how or why they impacted on the planning and leading of the activities. Include a personal development plan that sets SMARTER targets for improvement and identifies the activities and opportunities you could access to help you improve. You should also discuss the barriers to your improvement.

Justify your SMARTER targets, giving reasons as to how the targets will improve your planning and leading of sports activities.

Assessment criteria

Level 2 Pass	Level 2 Merit	Level 3 Distinction
Learning aim A: Know the attributes associated with successful sports leadership		
2A.P1 Describe, using relevant examples, the attributes required for, and responsibilities of, sports leadership.	**2A.M1** Explain the attributes required for, and responsibilities of, sports leadership.	
2A.P2 Describe the attributes of two selected successful sports leaders.	**2A.M2** Evaluate the attributes of two successful sports leaders.	**2A.D1** Compare and contrast the attributes of two successful sports leaders.
Learning aim B: Undertake the planning and leading of sports activities		
2B.P3 Plan two selected sports activities.	**2B.M3** Justify the choice of activities within the sports activity plan.	
2B.P4 Independently lead a sports activity session.	**2B.M4** Lead a successful sports activity session.	
Learning aim C: Review the planning and leading of sports activities		
2C.P5 Review the planning and leading of the sports activity session, describing strengths and areas for improvement, and targets for future development as a sports leader.	**2C.M5** Explain targets for future development as a sports leader, including a personal development plan.	**2C.D2** Justify targets for future development as a sports leader and activities within the personal development plan.

Knowledge recap answers

Learning aim A, page 11

1. Sports coaches, fitness instructors, school/college coaches, local club coaches, national club coaches and amateur coaches.
2. Good communication skills, organisation of equipment, knowledge, activity structure, target setting, use of language, personal appearance, enthusiasm, confidence and motivational skills. The leader should also have good humour and personality. They should be able to evaluate performance and use a range of leadership styles for different circumstances.
3. Sports leaders need to show good professional conduct and have an excellent knowledge of health and safety issues. The leader should treat everyone with equality. The leader has certain legal responsibilities regarding insurance and child protection. Leaders should behave ethically and uphold certain values, and ensure that the rules and regulations of the sport are applied fairly and consistently.

Learning aim B, page 35

1. A warm up should consist of a steady pulse-raising activity followed by some mobility work that stretches the major muscles that will be used in the session. The warm up should be completed with a sport-specific activity to prepare the participant for the activities planned for the session.
2. The purposes of a cool down are to promote recovery by removing waste products and to slowly return the body to pre-exercise levels.
3. The needs of the participants should be considered. People of different ages, abilities and gender will have different requirements. Attention should also be paid to medical issues. The number of participants will also affect your planning of the use of resources. It is important to set SMARTER goals for the session to ensure your aims and objectives are met. Once you know about your participants you can plan the effective use of your resources such as equipment, time and environment. Finally, it is of utmost importance that the health and safety considerations are met. A risk assessment should be completed and informed consent should be gained from the participants.

Learning aim C, Topic C.1, page 47

1. Feedback can be received from participants in the form of questionnaires and comment cards. Verbal and written feedback can be provided by observers such as teachers, peers or other sports leaders. Sessions can also be recorded and played back after the session for thorough analysis.

Learning aim C, Topic C.2, page 48

1. A personal development plan should identify strengths and areas of improvement. The plan should also set SMARTER targets for the areas that need improving. In addition to this the sports leader should describe the opportunities and potential barriers to the targets that have been set.
2.
   - Cost – The cost of coaching courses may be too much which will limit my opportunity to development my technical knowledge of the sport.
   - Geographical location – There may be no resources in my local area to access to help me to improve e.g. no facilities.
   - Time – I could be too busy with other commitments to spend time improving my leadership skills e.g. a full time job.
   - Gender – Some sports are still heavily influenced by men and it may be difficult to get the opportunity to lead these activities e.g. rugby.
   - Cultural differences – in some cultures, involvement in sport activities is frowned upon for certain individuals e.g. in Muslim communities female participation in sports is very low.